W0272027

Aus der Reihe:
English - quite easy

Friedhelm Heitmann

All about teenagers

Band 6

Übungsmaterial zum Einsatz im elementaren Förderunterricht zum Erlernen der englischen Sprache

Lernen mit Erfolg
KOHL VERLAG
Der Verlag mit dem Baum
www.kohlverlag.de

Nutzen Sie unseren bequemen Onlineshop!

• Ausführliche Informationen
• Aussagekräftige Leseproben
• Schnäppchen & besondere Angebote

www.kohlverlag.de

English - quite easy (Band 6)
- All about teenagers -

1. Auflage 2009

© Kohl-Verlag, Kerpen 2009

Inhalt: Friedhelm Heitmann
Grafik & Satz: Kohl-Verlag
Druck: Orths Medien GmbH

Bestell-Nr. 10 940

ISBN: 3-86632-940-7
ISBN-13: 978-3-86632-940-9

Inhalt

KOHL VERLAG Der Verlag mit dem Baum www.kohlverlag.de
English: quite easy / Band 6
All about teenagers - Bestell-Nr. 10 940

Vorwort

Liebe Kolleginnen und Kollegen,

Englisch ist eine Weltsprache, man kann sie auch als „Weltsprache Nr. 1“ bezeichnen. Weltweit wird in der englischen Sprache im privaten und öffentlichen Leben kommuniziert. Englisch ist in vielfältigen Lebenssituationen anzutreffen. Diese Sprache gilt als leicht zu erlernende Sprache, zumindest wird dies wiederholt behauptet. Der Schulalltag zeigt jedoch: Manche Schülerinnen und Schüler haben große Schwierigkeiten mit dem Englischen.

Vor diesem Hintergrund entstand die von mir verfasste Reihe „English - quite easy“, in der in kleinen Schritten „step by step“ vorgegangen wird. Die vorliegenden Bände sind vorgesehen für Anfänger, sie sind konzipiert für den elementaren Förderunterricht. Die dargebotenen Arbeitsblätter gingen aus der Schulpraxis hervor – und zwar aus der langjährigen Arbeit mit Haupt- und Förderschülern. Diese verfügten zunächst – bei Beginn des Unterrichts – über keine oder nur geringe Englischkenntnisse.

Die vorliegenden Kopiervorlagen sind jederzeit veränder- und erweiterbar. Weitere Anregungen sind dabei gern willkommen.

Viel Freude und Erfolg beim Einsatz der vorliegenden Kopiervorlagen wünschen Ihnen der Kohl-Verlag und

Friedhelm Heitmann

Die Reihe „English – quite easy“ besteht bisher aus folgenden sechs Bänden:

- **<u>Band 1</u>: Let‘s start to speak English** **Nr. 10 805** **12,90 €**
- **<u>Band 2</u>: Let‘s go on speaking English** **Nr. 10 806** **12,90 €**
- **<u>Band 3</u>: Grammar for beginners** **Nr. 10 848** **12,90 €**
- **<u>Band 4</u>: From Germany to the United Kingdom** **Nr. 10 849** **12,90 €**
- **<u>Band 5</u>: All about jobs** **Nr. 10 939** **14,90 €**
- **<u>Band 6</u>: All about teenagers** **Nr. 10 940** **13,90 €**

Didaktische und methodische Hinweise

Die präsentierten Bände dienen der Vermittlung, Festigung und Überprüfung elementarer Grundkenntnisse der englischen Sprache. Je nach Bedarf oder Wunsch lassen sich die Bände ganz oder in Auszügen (Schwerpunkte daraus bzw. einzelne Seiten) verwenden. Die Werke eignen sich in kompletter Form für Schülerinnen und Schüler im herkömmlichen Unterricht sowie im Rahmen der Wochenplanarbeit und Freiarbeit. Sowohl für einzelne Schülerinnen und Schüler als auch für die gesamte Klasse können die direkt einsetzbaren Vorlagen benutzt werden.

Einerseits sind die Arbeitsblätter gewöhnlich schnell überschaubar, zum anderen bieten sie genügend Platz für schriftliche Eintragungen. Die Schülerinnen und Schüler benötigen dafür keine weiteren Einzelblätter, Schreibblöcke oder Hefte. Auf vielen Arbeitsblättern werden als Hilfestellung beispielsweise Satzanfänge oder ungeordnete Lösungshinweise vorgegeben.

Im Anschluss an die Arbeitsblätter gibt es in jedem Band zwei Leistungskontrollen, die im Unterricht als Tests oder Klassenarbeiten eingesetzt werden können. Dabei können jeweils 100 Punkte erzielt werden.

Im Anhang zum Band sind die Lösungen zu den einzelnen Arbeitsblättern und Leistungskontrollen aufgelistet. Ideal ist es, wenn der Lehrer/die Lehrerin den Schülerinnen und Schülern die Gelegenheit gibt, ihre Antworten selbst im Anhang zu überprüfen.

Genug der Vorbemerkungen! Die folgenden Materialien sprechen für sich, sodass ganz bewusst auf weitere didaktische und methodische Anmerkungen verzichtet wird. Letztlich bleibt es den Lehrerinnen und Lehrern überlassen, welche der hier vorgestellten Materialien sie in den Unterricht aufnehmen.

1 All about you

Exercise 1: *Translate the 20 characteristics into German. Look at yourself. How is your character like? Mark it with a cross.*

		not 1	a little 2	unde-cided 3	much 4	very much 5
a) attractive =						
b) vain =						
c) clever =						
d) tidy =						
e) friendly =						
f) polite =						
g) fair =						
h) helpful =						
i) reliable =						
j) hard-working =						
k) honest =						
l) reserved =						
m) shy =						
n) sensitive =						
o) romantic =						
p) curious =						
q) brave =						
r) amusing =						
s) jolly =						
t) wild =						

Exercise 2: *What do your classmates and friends think about you?*

KOHL VERLAG Der Verlag mit dem Baum www.kohlverlag.de
English: quite easy / Band 6
All about teenagers - Bestell-Nr. 10 940

2 Feelings

Feelings attend us. You can have good and bad feelings.

Exercise 1: *Which of the following feelings are good and which of them are bad?*

happy - sad - nervous - funny - lucky - proud - bored - in love - angry - disappointed

good feelings: ______________________________

bad feelings: ______________________________

Exercise 2: *Write down another two good and bad feelings.*

good feelings: ______________ bad feelings: ______________

Exercise 3: *What is your "feeling factor" at this moment?*

-5 -4 -3 -2 -1 0 1 2 3 4 5

My feeling factor is ______________________ .

Explain your feeling: I feel ______________________

____

Exercise 4: *When do you have good feelings? Give 3 examples.*

____

____

____

____

____

KOHL VERLAG Der Verlag mit dem Baum www.kohlverlag.de
English: quite easy / Band 6
All about teenagers - Bestell-Nr. 10 940

2 Feelings

Exercise 5: *When do you have bad feelings? Give 3 examples.*

Exercise 6: *Imagine, you have bad feelings. What could you do to feel better?*

Exercise 7: *"A person without any feelings." – What does it mean?*

Exercise 8: *What is the opposite of* **feeling**? *Answer in a complete sentence.*

English: quite easy / Band 6
All about teenagers - Bestell-Nr. 10 940
KOHL VERLAG
www.kohlverlag.de

3 Problems

Life is like a roller coaster. You have good times, but you also have bad times.

Exercise 1: *Which people causes you troubles?*

Sometimes I have troubles with ... ____________________________

____

____

Exercise 2: *Do you have any problems at the moment? Did you have any problems in the past?*

At the moment I have ... ____________________________

____

In the past I ... ____________________________

____

Exercise 3: *Describe a problem.*

____

____

Exercise 4: *What can you do if you have a problem?*

- You can talk to ... ____________________________ .
- You can cry ... ____________________________ .
- You can listen to ... ____________________________ .
- You can play ... ____________________________ .
- You can go ... ____________________________ .

What do you do if you have a problem?

____

KOHL VERLAG Der Verlag mit dem Baum www.kohlverlag.de
English: quite easy / Band 6
All about teenagers - Bestell-Nr. 10 940

4 Differences between girls and boys

Exercise 1: *Which of the following attributes are typical for girls and which of them are typical for boys? Fill in and translate into German.*

work harder at school - are heavier - pay more attention to their clothes - are more romantic - are more aggressive - are stronger - are taller - cannot give birth to babies - can run faster - cause more troubles - get better marks at school - have a clitoris - have a penis - have a vagina - have a womb - have egg cells - have longer hair - have more muscles - have sperms - have testicles - have breasts - love dancing - play football - use less cosmetics - ...

Girls	Boys

Exercise 2: *Do you know more differences between girls and boys? Write down:*

English: quite easy / Band 6
All about teenagers - Bestell-Nr. 10 940
KOHL VERLAG
www.kohlverlag.de

5 A picture

Exercise 1: *Describe: What do you see in the picture? What could be the situation? What do the boy and the girl talk about?*

a) In the picture you see ______________________________

____

b) The girl ______________________________

c) The boy ______________________________

d) They ______________________________

____

e) The __________ says: ______________________________

f) The __________ answers: ______________________________

g) Behind the girl ______________________________

____

h) On the right side of the picture ______________________________

____

i) The dog ______________________________

j) In the sky the sun ______________________________

KOHL VERLAG Der Verlag mit dem Baum www.kohlverlag.de
English: quite easy / Band 6
All about teenagers - Bestell-Nr. 10 940

6 The boy/girl of my dreams

Exercise 1: *Complete the sentences.*

a) Her/His name is ... ______________________________

b) He/She comes from ... ______________________________

c) His/Her hair is ... ______________________________

d) The colour of his/her eyes ... ______________________________

e) He/She has (got) ... ______________________________

____

f) His/Her figure is ... ______________________________

____

g) He/She wears ... ______________________________

____

h) Our hobbies are ... ______________________________

____

____

i) We don‘t like ... ______________________________

____

____

j) The nickname of my darling is ... ______________________________

k) I call my darling ... ______________________________

____

l) We want to ...

____

Exercise 2: *Write down more informations about the person of your dreams.*

____

____

____

English: quite easy / Band 6
All about teenagers - Bestell-Nr. 10 940
KOHL VERLAG Der Verlag mit dem Baum
www.kohlverlag.de

7 Looking for a boyfriend/girlfriend

Exercise 1: **a)** *How should your boyfriend/girlfriend look like?*

My boyfriend/girlfriend should ... ______________________________

____

b) *Where can you meet a boyfriend/girlfriend?*

You can meet ... ______________________________

____

____

c) *How are you dressed if you are looking for a boyfriend/girlfriend?*

I wear ... ______________________________

____

d) *What can you say if you are interested in a boy/girl?*

You can say ... ______________________________

____

e) *What could you do with a boy/girl?*

You could ... ______________________________

____

____

f) *What present could you give to your boyfriend/girlfriend?*

You can give ... ______________________________

____

g) *How can you say goodbye to a boyfriend/girlfriend?*

You can say ... ______________________________

____

KOHL VERLAG Der Verlag mit dem Baum
English: quite easy / Band 6
All about teenagers - Bestell-Nr. 10 940
www.kohlverlag.de

8 In love

Exercise 1: *Translate the following phrases into German. This might be the start of a conversation.*

a) "Excuse me, can you help me?"

____

b) "Can you tell me what time it is?"

____

c) "Are you here for the first time?"

____

d) "Would you like a drink?"

____

e) "Would you like to dance?"

____

f) "Do you have a little time for me?"

____

g) "You have got beautiful eyes!"

____

h) "May I see you again?"

____

i) "May I ask you for your telephone number?"

____

j) "Would you like to go for a walk?"

____

KOHL VERLAG Der Verlag mit dem Baum www.kohlverlag.de
English: quite easy / Band 6
All about teenagers - Bestell-Nr. 10 940

Exercise 2: *You can call your darling: My ... (Translate into German.)*

a) darling ⇨ ____________________

b) honey ⇨ ____________________

c) candy ⇨ ____________________

d) bunny ⇨ ____________________

e) sweetheart ⇨ ____________________

f) baby ⇨ ____________________

g) sugar ⇨ ____________________

h) mouse ⇨ ____________________

i) sweetie ⇨ ____________________

j) sugar baby ⇨ ____________________

Exercise 3: *You can tell your darling: (Translate into German.)*

a) I need you. ____________________

b) I love you. ____________________

c) I like you very much. ____________________

d) You are the boy/girl of my dreams. ____________________

e) You are the prettiest girl in the world. ____________________

f) You are very attractive. ____________________

g) I want to kiss you all the time.

____

h) I am crazy about you. ____________________

i) It‘s very nice to be with you.

____

j) I want to be with you day and night.

____

KOHL VERLAG Der Verlag mit dem Baum www.kohlverlag.de
English: quite easy / Band 6
All about teenagers - Bestell-Nr. 10 940

8 In love

Exercise 4: *You can surprise your darling with the following rhymes (translate into German).*

a) Your eyes are blue,
and I need you.

b) It‘s really true:
I love you.

c) Just from the start
you are in my heart.

d) Your lips are red, can‘t get
you out of my head.

e) You look so fine –
will you be mine?

f) .....

Exercise 5: *Another popular rhyme:*

Roses are red,
violets are blue,
sugar is sweet,
and so are you.

Search for other (popular) rhymes and write them down.

9 All about love

Exercise 1: *Complete the following 10 sentences and translate them into German.*

a) People fall in ... .

b) Love is ... .

c) There are many ... .

d) A popular love song is ... .

e) If you are in love, you ... .

f) You can write ... .

g) Some people like ... .

h) You can say ... .

i) It may be that ... .

j) Two people who love each other can ... .

Exercise 2: *Write down more sentences about love and translate them into German.*

KOHL VERLAG Der Verlag mit dem Baum www.kohlverlag.de
English: quite easy / Band 6
All about teenagers - Bestell-Nr. 10 940

10 Sex

Exercise 1: *Translate the text into the German language.*

Two people who love each other usually want to have sex together. People have sex for pleasure and/or to make babies. Sex usually starts with kisses and necking. Both partners cuddle each other closely (foreplay). So the man's penis becomes erected, the woman's vagina becomes moist. Now the penis can penetrate into the vagina. This is called "sexual intercourse". Petting means: The partners cuddle each other closely without the penis getting into the vagina.

When the man gets an ejaculation, the sperms might come together with an egg cell. In this case the woman gets pregnant and she will have a baby. Especially young people often don't want to have babies. There are several ways to prevent a pregnany. For example: the man can use a condom, the woman can take the pill.

Sex can be a wonderful feeling. But there are some risks. Having sex with a new partner can be dangerous. You might infect yourself with AIDS (that means: Acquired Immune Deficiency Syndrome). AIDS is a very serious disease which leads to death. So be careful and use condoms!

KOHL VERLAG Der Verlag mit dem Baum www.kohlverlag.de
English: quite easy / Band 6
All about teenagers - Bestell-Nr. 10 940

11 Love and sex

<u>Exercise 1</u>: *What do you know about love and sex? Write down 15 complete sentences.*

English: quite easy / Band 6 - Bestell-Nr. 10 940
All about teenagers
KOHL VERLAG Der Verlag mit dem Baum
www.kohlverlag.de

12 A teenager

Bob is a pupil and 15 years old. He has one single interest in school and at work: Bob makes himself comfortable. You can say: He is lazy. The teenager gets aggressive very quickly. Sometimes he even offends or insults other people. He loves watching horror videos on TV and playing bloody computer games. Bob hangs around with other youths. ...

Exercise 1: *Write down more about Bob and his clique. Imagine how they spend their time. What may happen?*

Exercise 2: *What do you think of Bob? Write down your opinion.*

Exercise 3: *What do you think about "Violence is no solution."?*

13 The clique

Teenagers spend most of their time with their friends. They can have a lot of fun, but also some problems. Sometimes the clique is for teens more important than the own family.

Exercise 1: **a)** *With your friends you can talk about anything. Write down some topics you and your friends talk about.*

- ______________________________
- ______________________________
- ______________________________
- ______________________________
- ______________________________

b) *Teenagers do many things. Examples:*

- ______________________________
- ______________________________
- ______________________________
- ______________________________

c) *Sometimes teenagers do bad things. Examples:*

- ______________________________
- ______________________________
- ______________________________
- ______________________________

d) *There may be conflicts between teenagers. Examples:*

- ______________________________
- ______________________________
- ______________________________

Last but not least:

The television often sends bad reports of “todays teenagers“. “Alcohol“, “violence“, “senselessnes“ are popular words in newspaper headlines. However, teens are not so bad. We should not loose our confidence.

English: quite easy / Band 6
All about teenagers - Bestell-Nr. 10 940
www.kohlverlag.de

14 Puberty

Exercise 1: *Translate the text into the German language.*

Puberty is a time of development. Your body changes from being a child to being an adult. It‘s a stage with several changes and problems. The female breast starts growing. Young women begin to menstruate. The male voice gets deeper (vocal change). The testicles of young men start producing sperms.

Following things often happen in the puberty:

- You fall in love.
- You are lovesick.
- You begin to smoke cigarettes.
- You begin to drink alcohol.
- You come home too late.
- You have quarrels with your parents.
- You want to move away from home.
- You lose interest in school.
- You have trouble with other teenagers.
- You get in contact with the police.
- ...

KOHL VERLAG Der Verlag mit dem Baum www.kohlverlag.de
English: quite easy / Band 6
All about teenagers - Bestell-Nr. 10 940

14 Puberty

Exercise 2: *Answer the questions:*

a) What means “puberty“?

b) What changes happen to girls in puberty?

c) *What changes happen to boys in puberty?*

d) *Write down 5 things which often happen in puberty:*

e) *Which are your problems in the age of puberty?*

English: quite easy / Band 6
All about teenagers - Bestell-Nr. 10 940
www.kohlverlag.de

15 # "Yesterday" – a famous Beatles' song

Exercise 1: *Do you understand the following song? Translate into German.*

Yesterday, ______
all my troubles seemed so far away: ______
now it looks as though they're ______
here to stay. ______
Oh I believe in yesterday. ______
Suddenly, ______
I'm not half the man I used to be: ______
there's a shadow hanging over me. ______
Oh, yesterday came suddenly. ______
Why she had to go, ______
I don't know: ______
He wouldn't say, ______
I said something wrong, ______
now I long for yesterday. ______
Yesterday ______
love was such an easy game to play: ______
now I need a place to hide away. ______
Oh, I believe in yesterday. ______
Why she had to go, ______
I don't know: ______
He wouldn't say. ______
I said something wrong, ______
now I long for yesterday. ______
Yesterday, ______
love was such an easy game to play; ______
now I need a place to hide away. ______
Oh, I believe in yesterday. ______
Yesterday ______

KOHL VERLAG Der Verlag mit dem Baum www.kohlverlag.de
English: quite easy / Band 6
All about teenagers - Bestell-Nr. 10 940

16 The charts

Vorschlag: Jeder Schüler erstellt zunächst für sich eine Hitliste englischsprachlicher Titel. Anschließend wird in der Kasse gemeinsam über die Platzierungen der genannten englischsprachlichen Titel abgestimmt.

Ranks:	Title of the song	Singer / Group:
Top 1		
	That means in German:	
Top 2		
	That means in German:	
Top 3		
	That means in German:	
Top 4		
	That means in German:	
Top 5		
	That means in German:	
Top 6		
	That means in German:	
Top 7		
	That means in German:	
Top 8		
	That means in German:	
Top 9		
	That means in German:	
Top 10		
	That means in German:	

17 My star – a guessing game

Exercise 1: *Write down 10 hints:*

1. hint: ______________________________
2. hint: ______________________________
3. hint: ______________________________
4. hint: ______________________________
5. hint: ______________________________
6. hint: ______________________________
7. hint: ______________________________
8. hint: ______________________________
9. hint: ______________________________
10. hint: ______________________________

Answer (My star's name): ______________________________

Questions: *Write down ten questions which you would ask your star!*

1. ______________________________ ?
2. ______________________________ ?
3. ______________________________ ?
4. ______________________________ ?
5. ______________________________ ?
6. ______________________________ ?
7. ______________________________ ?
8. ______________________________ ?
9. ______________________________ ?
10. ______________________________ ?

KOHL VERLAG Der Verlag mit dem Baum www.kohlverlag.de
English: quite easy / Band 6
All about teenagers - Bestell-Nr. 10 940

18 Media

Teenagers are very interested in media, especially in new media.

Exercise 1: *Write down the names of ten media.*
Complete the missing letters.

a) b o __ __ in German: ____________

b) n e __ __ __ __ __ __ __ in German: ____________

c) m a __ __ __ __ __ __ in German: ____________

d) t e __ __ __ __ __ __ __ in German: ____________

e) m o __ __ __ __ __ __ __ __ __ in German: ____________

f) r a __ __ __ in German: ____________

g) t e __ __ __ __ __ __ __ __ in German: ____________

h) c o __ __ __ __ __ __ in German: ____________

i) v i __ __ __ __ __ __ __ __ __ __ __ in German: ____________

j) C D __ __ __ __ __ __ in German: ____________

Exercise 2: **a)** *Write down three print media:*

____

____

____

b) *Write down three new media:*

____

____

____

c) *Do you like print media?*

____

____

KOHL VERLAG Der Verlag mit dem Baum www.kohlverlag.de
English: quite easy / Band 6
All about teenagers - Bestell-Nr. 10 940

d) *Do you like new media?*

e) *Which media do you use?*

f) *Make a ranking list of the media which you use. Which is your favourite media?*

Pros and cons of media:

Exercise 3: *Translate the following ten sentences into German.*

a) You can get a lot of informations in a short time.

b) People can become aggressive.

c) You can get addicted to media.

d) Media offer entertainment, excitement and diversion.

e) Buying and using of media cost money.

f) Some people loose contact to reality, they live in a virtual world.

KOHL VERLAG Der Verlag mit dem Baum www.kohlverlag.de
English: quite easy / Band 6
All about teenagers - Bestell-Nr. 10 940

g) Media make people's life easier (telecommuting, teleshopping, ..)

____

h) You are reachable at any place and any time (mobile phone ...).

____

i) Social contacts between people get lost.

____

j) Computer is high technology.

____

Exercise 4: *Which sentences are advantages of media (= pros)?*
Which sentences are disadvantages of media (= cons)?

Advantages of media (= pros)	Disadvantages of media (= cons)

KOHL VERLAG Der Verlag mit dem Baum www.kohlverlag.de
English: quite easy / Band 6
All about teenagers - Bestell-Nr. 10 940

19 Doing sport(s) - 10 reasons

Sport is good for ...

- ... health;
- ... thinking and learning;
- ... achieving success;
- ... your self-conficence;
- ... reducing stress and aggressions;
- ... education;

Sport gives you ...

- ... conversation and social contacts;
- ... experiences, events, adventures;
- ... diversion, entertainment and fun;

Sport is a wonderful leisure activity.

<u>Exercise 1</u>: *Translate into German.*

<u>Exercise 2</u>: **a)** *Which are the three most important reasons to do sports?*

b) *What kind of sport do you like? What kind of sport do you do?*

English: quite easy / Band 6
All about teenagers - Bestell-Nr. 10 940
KOHL VERLAG Der Verlag mit dem Baum
www.kohlverlag.de

20 Leisure time

In your leisure time you can do lots of funny things.

Exercise 1: *What can you do? Complete the following sentences.*

Answers:

animals - basketball - a bicycle - a card-game - a coffee - computer games - a date - football - friends - to a concert - the guitar - relax - a horse - listen to some music - a museum - a party - shopping - swimming - television - on a trip - for a walk - dinner with friends - to the cinema - work in the garden

a) You can go ______________________

b) You can go ______________________

c) You can go ______________________

d) You can go ______________________

e) You can play ______________________

f) You can play ______________________

g) You can have ______________________

h) You can have ______________________

i) You can ride ______________________

j) You can visit ______________________

k) You can watch ______________________

l) You can do ______________________

m) You can ______________________

n) You can go ______________________

o) You can go ______________________

p) You can play ______________________

q) You can play ______________________

r) You can play ______________________

s) You can have ______________________

t) You can have ______________________

u) You can ride ______________________

v) You can meet ______________________

w) You can watch ______________________

x) You can do ______________________

KOHL VERLAG Der Verlag mit dem Baum
www.kohlverlag.de
English: quite easy / Band 6
All about teenagers - Bestell-Nr. 10 940

Exercise 2: *Do you have more ideas what to do in your leisure time?*

I can ...

Exercise 3: *Which are your favourite activities in your spare time?*

I like to ...

Exercise 4: *Are there any things you don't like to do at all?*

I don't like to ...

21 My hobby

Exercise 1: *Translate the text into German.*

Above all I like football. It is my life. I play football in a youth team. The name of my club is HEBC. Two times a week I go to the football training. At weekends I usually have league matches, cup ties or friendly games. I am a forward, but no goalgetter. Sometimes we win, on other days we lose or draw. In my spare time I also play football in the park near our house. Besides I often watch football matches on television. Sometimes my dad and I go to the stadium to see a match with my favourite football club “Hamburger SV“. My favourite football club is the Hamburger SV. I like the player Paulo Guerrero, but I think: At present Cristiano Ronaldo is the best football player in the world.

Exercise 2: *Do you like football, too? Write down sentences about football or your personal hobby (5 sentences at least).*

KOHL VERLAG Der Verlag mit dem Baum
www.kohlverlag.de
English: quite easy / Band 6
All about teenagers - Bestell-Nr. 10 940

22 A party

Exercise 1: *Let's have a party.*

1. The party takes place on (date): ____________________
2. The party begins at (time): ____________________
3. It is in (place) ____________________
4. The motto of the party is: ____________________
5. You can eat: ____________________
6. You can drink: ____________________
7. You can listen to: ____________________
8. You can dance: ____________________
9. You can sing: ____________________
10. You can watch: ____________________
11. You can meet: ____________________
12. You can talk about: ____________________
13. You can play: ____________________
14. You can laugh about: ____________________

We wish: ____________________

KOHL VERLAG Der Verlag mit dem Baum www.kohlverlag.de
English: quite easy / Band 6 - Bestell-Nr. 10 940
All about teenagers

23 My last weekend

Exercise 1: *Complete the following 10 sentences.*

a) My last weekend was ... ____________________

b) The weather was ... ____________________

c) On Saturday .. ____________________

d) Then ... ____________________

e) Later on ... ____________________

f) On Sunday morning ... ____________________

g) Next ... ____________________

h) After that ... ____________________

i) In the evening ... ____________________

j) The best thing of the weekend .. ____________________

Exercise 2: *Write down more sentences.*

English: quite easy / Band 6
All about teenagers - Bestell-Nr. 10 940
www.kohlverlag.de

24 Personal hygiene and cosmetics

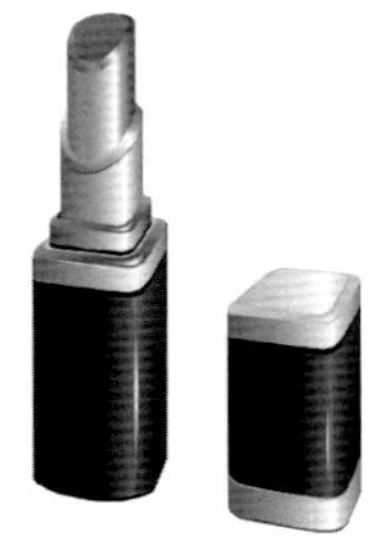

Exercise 1: *Cosmetics – what do the following words mean in German?*

a) soap ____________

b) tooth paste ____________

c) shampoo ____________

d) hairspray ____________

e) hair tonic ____________

f) setting lotion ____________

g) shaving cream ____________

h) body spray ____________

i) face cream ____________

j) facial tonic ____________

k) eyeliner ____________

l) lipstick ____________

m) nail polish remover ____________

n) cream ____________

o) mouthwash ____________

p) shower gel ____________

q) hair gel ____________

r) hair colour ____________

s) hair remover ____________

t) aftershave ____________

u) make-up ____________

v) face powder ____________

w) mascara ____________

x) eyeshadow ____________

y) nail polish ____________

Exercise 2: *Which cosmetics do you use?*

I use ... ____

____

____

____

____

____

English: quite easy / Band 6 - Bestell-Nr. 10 940
All about teenagers
KOHL VERLAG Der Verlag mit dem Baum
www.kohlverlag.de

24 Personal hygiene and cosmetics

Exercise 3: *What do you think about piercings, tattoos and body paintings?*

I ... ______________________________

____

____

____

____

Exercise 4: *What do you do in the bathroom?*

a) I wash ______________________________

b) I brush ______________________________

c) I put on ______________________________

d) I dye ______________________________

e) I comb ______________________________

f) I shave ______________________________

g) I rinse ______________________________

h) I cut ______________________________

i) I put on ______________________________

English: quite easy / Band 6
All about teenagers - Bestell-Nr. 10 940
KOHL VERLAG Der Verlag mit dem Baum
www.kohlverlag.de

25 Fashion and clothes

Exercise 1: **a)** *Are you interested in the new fashion?*

b) *How often do you go shopping?*

c) *What colours do you like?*

d) *What clothes do you like to wear?*

e) *What do these international sizes mean?*

XS = ______ L = ______

S = ______ XL = ______

M = ______ XXL = ______

f) *Which is your size?* ______

g) *What clothes you don't like to wear?*

h) *Are you interested in fashion shows?*

i) *Would you like to be a fashion model?*

j) *In Germany we say: "Good clothes open all doors." What does this slogan mean?*

English: quite easy / Band 6 - Bestell-Nr. 10 940
All about teenagers
KOHL VERLAG
www.kohlverlag.de

26 Health

Exercise 1: *What is good for your health?*
What is bad for your health? Write down:

- smoking cigarettes
- going for sports
- eating fruits
- going to the doctor.
- playing computer games every day
- overweight reducing
- ...
- eating lots of chips
- drinking alcohol
- riding a bicycle
- drinking coke
- watching TV all day long
- eating vegetables
- ....

Good for health:	Bad for health:

Exercise 2: **a)** *What other things are good for health? Write down.*

b) *What other things are bad for health? Write down.*

English: quite easy / Band 6
All about teenagers - Bestell-Nr. 10 940
KOHL VERLAG Der Verlag mit dem Baum
www.kohlverlag.de

Exercise 3: *What do you do for your health? Write down.*

Exercise 4: *A rhyme: „An apple a day keeps the doctor away.“ What does it mean?*

Exercise 5: *What can you eat to stay healthy?*

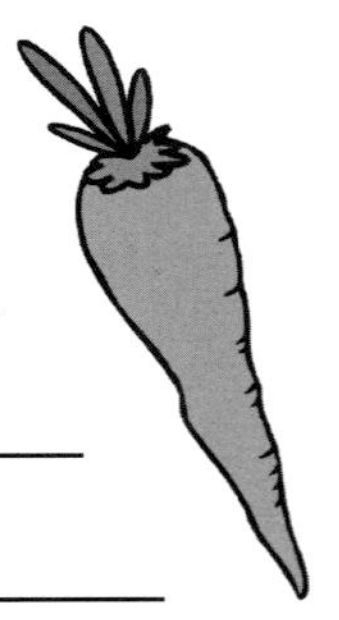

English: quite easy / Band 6
All about teenagers - Bestell-Nr. 10 940
KOHL VERLAG Der Verlag mit dem Baum
www.kohlverlag.de

27 Class test 1

Name: ______________________ Date: ______________________

Exercise 1: Your characteristics – *write down 10 characteristics:*

______________________ ______________________

______________________ ______________________

______________________ ______________________

______________________ ______________________

______________________ ______________________

Exercise 2: Feelings – *translate into English.*

a) nervös ⇨ ______________________

b) böse ⇨ ______________________

c) traurig ⇨ ______________________

d) gelangweilt ⇨ ______________________

e) glücklich ⇨ ______________________

f) enttäuscht ⇨ ______________________

g) zufrieden ⇨ ______________________

h) lustig ⇨ ______________________

i) stolz ⇨ ______________________

j) verliebt ⇨ ______________________

Exercise 3: Problems – *you can have problems with:*

______________________ ______________________

______________________ ______________________

______________________ ______________________

______________________ ______________________

______________________ ______________________

English: quite easy / Band 6
All about teenagers - Bestell-Nr. 10 940
KOHL VERLAG
Der Verlag mit dem Baum
www.kohlverlag.de

Class test 1

Name: ______________________ Date: ______________________

Exercise 4: Differences between girls and boys.
Write down 10 differences between girls and boys.

Girls	Boys

Exercise 5: In love – *how can you start a conversation with a boy or a girl?*

- ____
- ____
- ____
- ____
- ____
- ____
- ____
- ____
- ____
- ____

KOHL VERLAG Der Verlag mit dem Baum www.kohlverlag.de
English: quite easy / Band 6 All about teenagers - Bestell-Nr. 10 940

Class test 1

Name: ______________________ Date: ______________________

Exercise 6: **Your darling** – *how can you call your darling? Write down 10 examples.*

______________________ ______________________

______________________ ______________________

______________________ ______________________

______________________ ______________________

______________________ ______________________

Exercise 7: **Rhymes about love** – *write down 10 short rhymes about love.*

- ______________________
- ______________________
- ______________________
- ______________________
- ______________________
- ______________________
- ______________________
- ______________________
- ______________________
- ______________________

Exercise 8: **Friends** – *with your friends you can talk about anything. Write down some topics you and your friends talk about.*

______________________ ______________________

______________________ ______________________

______________________ ______________________

______________________ ______________________

______________________ ______________________

KOHL VERLAG Der Verlag mit dem Baum
www.kohlverlag.de
English: quite easy / Band 6
All about teenagers - Bestell-Nr. 10 940

Class test 1

Name: ______________________ Date: ______________________

Exercise 9: All about love – *complete the following 10 sentences.*

a) People fall ... ____ .

b) Love is ... ____ .

c) A popular song about love is: ________________________________ .

d) You can ... ____ .

e) Some lovers ... ____ .

f) Other lovers ... ____ .

g) Two people ... ____ .

h) It may be ... ____ .

i) Sex ... ____ .

j) AIDS ... ____ .

Exercise 10: Puberty – *what changes happen to boys and girls in puberty?*

- ____
- ____
- ____
- ____
- ____
- ____
- ____
- ____
- ____
- ____

KOHL VERLAG Der Verlag mit dem Baum
www.kohlverlag.de
English: quite easy / Band 6
All about teenagers - Bestell-Nr. 10 940

28 Class test 2

Name: ______________________ Date: ______________________

Exercise 1: **Media** – *write down the names of 10 media.*

______________________ ______________________

______________________ ______________________

______________________ ______________________

______________________ ______________________

______________________ ______________________

Exercise 2: **Pros and cons of media.**
Complete the following sentences.

pros	cons
- Media offer ______________________	- Buying and ______________________
______________________	______________________
- You are ______________________	- People can ______________________
______________________	______________________
- Media make ______________________	- You can ______________________
______________________	______________________
- You can ______________________	- Social contacts ______________________
______________________	______________________
- Media demonstrate ______________________	- Some people loose ______________________
______________________	______________________

KOHL VERLAG Der Verlag mit dem Baum www.kohlverlag.de
English: quite easy / Band 6
All about teenagers - Bestell-Nr. 10 940

Class test 2

Name: ______________________ Date: ______________________

Exercise 3: **Your star** – *write down 10 sentences about your star.*

- ____
- ____
- ____
- ____
- ____
- ____
- ____
- ____
- ____
- ____

Exercise 4: **Questions** – *write down 10 sentences which you would ask your star.*

- ____
- ____
- ____
- ____
- ____
- ____
- ____
- ____
- ____
- ____

KOHL VERLAG Der Verlag mit dem Baum www.kohlverlag.de
English: quite easy / Band 6
All about teenagers - Bestell-Nr. 10 940

Class test 2

Name: ______________________ Date: ______________________

Exercise 5: **Sports** – *write down 10 reasons.*

a) Sport is good for ... ____ .

b) Sport is good for ... ____ .

c) Sport is good for ... ____ .

d) Sport is good for ... ____ .

e) Sport is good for ... ____ .

f) Sport is good for ... ____ .

g) Sport gives you ... ____ .

h) Sport gives you ... ____ .

i) Sport gives you ... ____ .

j) Sport is ... ____ .

Exercise 6: **Leisure time** – *what can you do in your leisure time?*

a) I can ... ____ .

b) I can ... ____ .

c) I can ... ____ .

d) I can ... ____ .

e) I can ... ____ .

f) I can ... ____ .

g) I can ... ____ .

h) I can ... ____ .

i) I can ... ____ .

j) I can ... ____ .

KOHL VERLAG Der Verlag mit dem Baum www.kohlverlag.de
English: quite easy / Band 6
All about teenagers - Bestell-Nr. 10 940

Class test 2

Name: ____________________ Date: ____________________

Exercise 7: Hobby – *write about your favourite hobby. Try to find 10 sentences.*

- ______________________________
- ______________________________
- ______________________________
- ______________________________
- ______________________________
- ______________________________
- ______________________________
- ______________________________
- ______________________________
- ______________________________

Exercise 8: A weekend – *write about a weekend. Complete the sentences.*

a) This weekend was ... ______________________________ .

b) The weather was ... ______________________________ .

c) On ... ______________________________ .

d) Then ... ______________________________ .

e) Later on ... ______________________________ .

f) On ... ______________________________ .

g) At lunchtime ... ______________________________ .

h) After that ... ______________________________ .

i) At last ... ______________________________ .

j) The best thing ... ______________________________ .

English: quite easy / Band 6
All about teenagers - Bestell-Nr. 10 940
KOHL VERLAG Der Verlag mit dem Baum
www.kohlverlag.de

Class test 2

Name: ______________________ Date: ______________________

Exercise 9: **Personal hygiene** – *how do you call the following items in English?*

a) Seife ____.

b) Creme ____.

c) Zahnpasta ____.

d) Duschgel ____.

e) Körperspray ____.

f) Rasierwasser ____.

g) Schminke ____.

h) Nagellack ____.

i) Lippenstift ____.

j) Haarfärbemittel ____.

Exercise 10: **Health** – *write down 5 things which are bad for health.*

a) ____.

b) ____.

c) ____.

d) ____.

e) ____.

Write down 5 things which are good for health.

f) ____.

g) ____.

h) ____.

i) ____.

j) ____.

KOHL VERLAG Der Verlag mit dem Baum www.kohlverlag.de
English: quite easy / Band 6
All about teenagers - Bestell-Nr. 10 940

29 The answers

1

1. **a)** attraktiv, anziehend; **b)** eingebildet, eitel; **c)** klug, schlau; **d)** sauber, ordentlich; **e)** freundlich; **f)** höflich; **g)** ehrlich; **h)** hilfsbereit, hilfreich; **i)** zuverlässig, vertrauenswürdig; **j)** fleißig, arbeitsam; **k)** ehrlich, aufrichtig; **l)** zurückhaltend, reserviert; **m)** scheu, schüchtern; **n)** sensibel, empfindlich; **o)** romantisch; **p)** neugierig, wissbegierig; **q)** mutig/tapfer; **r)** amüsant, unterhaltsam; **s)** lustig, fröhlich; **t)** wild

2

1. Good feelings: happy, funny, lucky, proud, in love Bad feelings: sad, nervous, disappointed, bored, angry
2. Good feelings: enthusiastic, friendly Bad feelings: listless, spiteful
3. I feel good, because the sun is shining.
4. I feel good when I don't have any homework. I feel good when I meet my friends. I feel good when I am in love.
5. I feel bad when I have to get up early. I feel bad when I have troubles with my mum. I feel bad when I have to do lots of things.
6. I can go to bed. I can listen to some music. I can talk to my best friend.
7. It means: The person is emotionally cold.
8. The opposite of feeling is the intellect.

3

1. Sometimes I have troubles with my father, my mother, my brother, my sister, my English teacher, my trainer, our neighbour, my friend or other pupils.
2. I have problems with my parents, because I came home late yesterday. In the past I had problems with my class teacher, because I didn't do my homework.
3. My girlfriend and I wanted to spend the night together at my home. My parents didn't allow it.
4. I can talk to my best friend. I can cry for help. I can listen to some music. I can play card-games. I can go the advisory board. I tell my parents about it or talk to my best friend.

4

1. Girls: work harder at school, pay more attention to their clothes, are more romantic, get better marks at school, have a clitoris, have a vagina, have a womb, have egg cells, have longer hair, have breasts, love dancing
   Boys: are heavier, are more aggressive, are stronger, cannot give birth to babies, can run faster, cause more troubles, have a penis, have more muscles, have sperms, have testicles, play football, use less cosmetics

5

1. **a)** ... young people, a girl and a boy. **b)** ... is sitting in the grass in front of a tree. **c)** ... is kneeling opposite to the girl. **d)** are talking to each other, because they are friends. **e)** The boy says: "Let's go swimming!" **f)** The girl answers: "That's a good idea!" **g)** ... there is a big tree. **h)** ... you can see a ball and a dog. **i)** ... is sleeping. **j)** ... is shining.

6

1. **a)** His/Her name is Susan Miller. **b)** She comes from Hamburg. **c)** Her hair is blond. **d)** The colour of her eyes is green. **e)** She has got one sister and one brother. **f)** His/Her figure is tall and slender. **g)** She wears modern clothes. **h)** Our hobbies are sports (football, swimming) and music. **i)** We don't like rainy weather. **j)** The nickname of my darling is Sue. **k)** I call my darling "sweetheart". **l)** We want to spend our summer holidays in Spain.
2. The girl of my dreams wants to become a model.

7

1. **a)** ... be good-looking, nice, honest, loyal ... **b)** ... a girlfriend at any place, for example at school, at the disco, at the railway station, on the road, in the shopping center ... **c)** ... modern, clean clothes. **d)** ... „Hello, my name is ..., What is your name?" **e)** ... talk to each other, go for a walk, go to see a movie in a cinema, go dancing ... **f)** ... him/her a flower bouquet, a ring, a photo, a CD ... **g)** ... „Good night, I will dream of you."

8

1. **a)** Entschuldigung, kannst du mir helfen? **b)** Kannst du mir sagen, wie spät es ist? **c)** Bist du zum ersten Mal hier? **d)** Möchtest du etwas trinken? **e)** Möchtest du tanzen? **f)** Hast du ein bisschen Zeit für mich? **g)** Du hast schöne Augen. **h)** Darf ich dich wiedersehen? **i)** Darf ich dich nach deiner Telefonnummer fragen? **j)** Würdest du gerne spazieren gehen?
2. **a)** Mein Liebling; **b)** Mein Schatz („Honig"); **c)** Mein(e) Süße(r); **d)** Mein Häschen; **e)** Mein Schatz, („süßes Herz"); **f)** Mein Schatz, Liebling („Baby"); **g)** Mein Schatz („Zucker"); **h)** Meine Maus; **i)** Mein(e) Süße(r); **j)** Mein „Zuckerbaby"
3. **a)** Ich brauche dich. **b)** Ich liebe dich. **c)** Ich mag dich sehr. **d)** Du bist das Mädchen/der Junge meiner Träume. **e)** Du bist das hübscheste Mädchen auf der ganzen Welt. **f)** Du bist sehr attraktiv. **g)** Ich möchte dich die ganze Zeit küssen. **h)** Ich bin verrückt nach dir. **i)** Es ist sehr schön, mit dir zusammen zu sein. **j)** Ich möchte Tag und Nacht mit dir zusammen sein.
4. **a)** Deine Augen sind blau, und ich brauche dich. **b)** Es ist wirklich wahr: Ich liebe dich. **c)** Schon von Anfang an bist du in meinem Herzen. **d)** Deine Lippen sind rot. Du gehst mir nicht aus dem Kopf. **e)** Du siehst schön aus. Willst du mit mir gehen?
5. Rosen sind rot, Veilchen sind blau, Zucker ist süß und so bist du.

   I love you forever, hope to loose you never.
   You are nice and kind, always in my mind.
   It's very fine, you are my sunshine.
   Baby, you are funny. I'd love you to be my bunny.
   You look so fine, will you be mine?

English: quite easy / Band 6
All about teenagers - Bestell-Nr. 10 940
KOHL VERLAG Der Verlag mit dem Baum
www.kohlverlag.de

The answers

9

1. **a)** People fall in love. Menschen verlieben sich. **b)** Love is wonderful. Liebe ist wunderbar. **c)** There are many songs about love. Es gibt viele Lieder über (die) Liebe. **d)** A popular love song is „Yesterday“. Ein bekanntes Liebeslied ist „Yesterday“ (Beatles). **e)** If you are in love, you are very happy. Wenn du verliebt bist, bist du sehr glücklich. **f)** You can write love letters and love poems. Man kann Liebesbriefe und Liebesgedichte schreiben. **g)** Some people like love stories. Manche Leute mögen Liebesgeschichten. **h)** You can say: „My sweetheart“. Du kannst „Mein Schatz“ sagen. **i)** It may be that you get lovesick. Es kann sein, dass du Liebeskummer bekommst. **j)** Two people who love each other can marry. Zwei Menschen, die einander lieben, können heiraten.
2. We know a lot of proverbs about love. For example: Love is blind. Make love, not war, ...
   Wir kennen viele Sprichwörter über die Liebe. Zum Beispiel: Liebe macht blind. Macht Liebe, nicht Krieg. ...

10

1. Sex. Zwei Menschen, die sich lieben, möchten normalerweise Sex miteinander haben. Menschen haben Sex zum Vergnügen und/oder um Babies zu bekommen. Sex beginnt üblicherweise mit Küssen (Knutschen). Beide Partner umarmen einander fest (Vorspiel). So richtet sich der Penis des Mannes auf, die Scheide der Frau wird feucht. Jetzt kann der Penis in die Scheide eindringen. Das nennt man „Sexualverkehr“. Petting bedeutet: Die Partner schmusen miteinander, ohne dass der Penis in die Scheide eindringt. Wenn der Mann einen Samenerguss bekommt, können die Spermien mit einer Eizelle zusammenkommen. In diesem Fall wird die Frau schwanger und wird ein Baby bekommen. Besonders junge Menschen möchten oft noch keine Babies. Es gibt zahlreiche Wege, eine Schwangerschaft zu verhüten. Zum Beispiel: Der Mann kann ein Kondom verwenden, die Frau kann die Pille nehmen. Sex kann ein wundervolles Gefühl sein. Aber es gibt auch Risiken! Mit einem neuen Partner Sex zu haben, kann gefährlich sein. Man kann sich dabei mit AIDS anstecken (einer erworbenen Immunschwäche-Krankheit). AIDS ist eine sehr ernste Erkrankung, die zum Tode führt. Also – seid vorsichtig und verwendet Kondome!

11

1. Many people are in love. Love is a wonderful feeling. There is “love at first sight“. A proverb says: “Love is blind.“ Another german proverb says: “The way to a man‘s heart leads to his stomach.“ The patron of lovers is VALENTINE, who was a christian bishop. Saint Valentine‘s Day is on 14th of February. Don‘t forget this day. On this day you should give a present to your darling. Two lovers usually want to have sex together. Sex usually begins with kisses (= necking). “Sexual intercourse“ means: the penis of the man penetrates into the vagina of the woman. When the man gets an ejaculation, the sperms might come together with an egg cell. In this case the woman gets pregnant and she will have a baby 9 months later. You should protect yourself against AIDS by using a condom.

12

1. Bob often comes to school too late or is absent during all lessons. He doesn‘t do his homework. Bob doesn‘t look for a job, he doesn‘t have any working experience. He is the leader of the group. Most members of his clique are well-known to the police. The police already observes Bob and some other young people of the clique. Bob is reported to the police several times (because of insult and bodily harm). The young people drink alcohol, smoke cigarettes and use other drugs.
2. I don‘t accept Bob‘s behavior: He has only little interest in school and work. Besides he is aggressive. Bob has to improve his behavior, otherwise he may become a criminal.
3. I think “Violence is no solution“ is quite right. To apply force will complicate the situation and you will get even more problems instead of solving them.

13

1. **a)** We talk about sports, friendship, love, school, events.
   b) They listen to music or play music, do sports, watch on TV films, chat on the internet, work for school
   c) drink alcohol, smoke cigarettes, use drugs (hashish, heroin, ..), smear walls, damage or destroy things
   d) Teens might be jealous of other teenagers. Some teenagers are very aggressive and harm others. Some teens take things away from other teens.

14

1. Pubertät. Die Pubertät ist eine Zeit der Entwicklung. Dein Körper verändert sich vom Kindsein zum Erwachsensein. Es ist ein Stadium mit zahlreichen Veränderungen und Problemen. Die weibliche Brust beginnt zu wachsen. Junge Frauen bekommen ihre Menstruation. Die männliche Stimme wird tiefer (Stimmbruch). Die Hoden junger Männer beginnen, Spermien zu produzieren. Folgende Dinge passieren oft in der Pubertät: - Du verliebst dich. - Du hast Liebeskummer. - Du beginnst zu rauchen. - Du beginnst, Alkohol zu trinken. - Du kommst zu spät nach Hause. - Du hast Streit mit deinen Eltern. - Du willst von zu Hause ausziehen. - Du verlierst das Interesse an der Schule. - Du hast Ärger mit anderen Teenagern. - Du kommst in Kontakt mit der Polizei.
2. **a)** Puberty is the time when your body changes from being a child to being an adult. **b)** The female breast starts growing. Young women begin to menstruate. **c)** The male voice gets deeper (vocal change). Young men start producing sperms. **d)** Girls and boys fall in love. They begin to smoke cigarettes and to drink alcohol. They come home late and have quarrel with their parents. Young people want to move away from home. Some loose interest in school. **e)** I have some problems with my parents, when I come home too late. My parents don‘t like that I smoke cigarettes. Sometimes I have troubles with my girl friend, because sometimes it is not easy to come to an agreement about what we do together.

15

1. Gestern, alle Probleme schienen so weit weg. Jetzt sieht es so aus, als ob sie hierbleiben wollen. Oh, ich denke an gestern! Plötzlich bin ich nicht halb der Mann, der ich früher war. Da hängt ein Schatten über mir, der gestern plötzlich kam. Warum musste sie gehen? Ich weiß es nicht. Er würde es nicht sagen. Ich sagte etwas Falsches, nun sehne ich mich nach gestern. Gestern war die Liebe ein so leichtes Spiel, nun brauche ich einen Platz, um mich zu verstecken. Oh, ich denke an gestern! Warum musste sie gehen? Ich weiß es nicht. Er würde es nicht sagen. Ich sagte etwas Falsches, nun sehne ich mich nach gestern. Gestern war die Liebe ein so leichtes Spiel, nun brauche ich einen Platz, um mich zu verstecken. Oh, ich denke an gestern. Gestern.

KOHL VERLAG Der Verlag mit dem Baum www.kohlverlag.de
English: quite easy / Band 6
All about teenagers - Bestell-Nr. 10 940

29 The answers

17

1. 1. hint: My star is born in 1977. 2. hint: The person has got no sisters and no brothers. 3. hint: Her native country is Columbia. 4. hint: She is a singer and song writer. 5. hint: Her talent is found at the age of 13. 6. hint: At first my star sang in Spanish, later on in English, too. 7. hint: Today the woman is a famous pop- and rockstar. 8. hint: She supports poor, helpless children. 9. hint: The last letter of her name is an "a". 10. hint: The first letter of her name is an „S".
Answer: Shakira
Questions: **1.** When is your birthday? **2.** Are you married? **3.** Where do you live now? **4.** What are your hobbies? **5.** What fashion do you like? **6.** Where do you spend your holidays? **7.** Did you like school? **8.** What is your favourite animal? **9.** What do you aim to do next? **10.** Do you enjoy being famous?

18

1. **a)** book (Buch); **b)** newspaper (Zeitung); **c)** magazine (Zeitschrift); **d)** telephone (Telefon); **e)** mobile phone (Handy); **f)** radio (Radio); **g)** television (Fernsehapparat); **h)** computer (Computer); **i)** video recorder (Videorekorder); **j)** CD player (CD-Spieler)

2. **a)** book, newspaper, magazine; **b)** computer, mobile phone, CD-player; **c)** No, I do not (= No, I don't). **d)** Yes, I do. **e)** I use the media television, mobile phone, computer, CD-player, MP3 player, I pod. **f)** 1. mobile phone, 2. computer, 3. television, ...

3. **a)** Man kann eine Menge Informationen in kurzer Zeit bekommen. **b)** Menschen können aggressiv werden. **c)** Man kann mediensüchtig werden. **d)** Medien bieten Unterhaltung, Spannung und Zerstreuung. **e)** Der Kauf und das Benutzen von Medien kosten Geld. **f)** Manche Menschen verlieren den Bezug zur Wirklichkeit, sie leben in einer Scheinwelt. **g)** Medien machen das Leben der Menschen leichter (Telekommunikation, Teleshopping, ..) **h)** Man ist an jedem Ort und jederzeit erreichbar (Handy, ...) **i)** Soziale Kontakte zwischen den Menschen gehen verloren. **j)** Computer sind höhere Technologie.

4. Advantages of media (= pros): You can get al lot of information in a short time. You are reachable at any place and any time. Media offer entertainmelt, excitement and diversion. Media make people's life easier. Computer is high technology.
Disadvantages of media (= cons): People can become aggressive. You can get addicted to media. Buying and using of media cost money. Some people loose contact to reality, they live in a virtual world. Social contacts between people get lost.

19

1. Sport ist gut für die Gesundheit, das Denken und Lernen, das Erzielen von Erfolg, dein Selbstvertrauen, das Reduzieren von Stress und Aggression, die Schulbildung. Sport gibt dir Unterhaltung und soziale Kontakte, Erfahrungen, Veranstaltungen und Abenteuer, Zeitvertreib, Unterhaltung und Spaß. Sport ist eine wunderbare Freizeitbeschäftigung!

2. **a)** Sport is very important für the human beings. You should do sport. There are several reasons. I think the three best reasons are: Sport is goog for health, social contacts and reducing stress.
b) I like and do the sports football, jogging and swimming.

20

1. **a)** for a walk; **b)** to a concert; **c)** shopping; **d)** to the cinema; **e)** computer games; **f)** basketball; **g)** dinner with friends; **h)** a date; **i)** a horse; **j)** a museum; **k)** television; **l)** work in the garden; **m)** listen to some music; **n)** on a trip; **o)** swimming; **p)** football; **q)** the guitar; **r)** a card-game; **s)** a coffee; **t)** a party; **u)** a bicycle; **v)** friends; **w)** animals; **x)** relax

2. I can listen to music, go dancing, go boating, fishing, go jogging, play table tennis, eat ice cream, read a book, write a letter ...

3. I like to play football, go swimming, meet friends, ...

4. I don't like to go shopping, go fishing, write a letter, ...

21

1. Mein Hobby. Vor allem mag ich Fußball. Er ist mein Leben. Ich spiele Fußball in einer Jugendmannschaft. Der Name des Vereins ist HEBC. Zweimal in der Woche gehe ich zum Fußballtraining. Am Wochenende sind gewöhnlich ein Punktspiele, Pokalspiele oder Freundschaftsspiele. Ich bin Stürmer, aber kein Torjäger. Manchmal gewinnen wir, an anderen Tagen verlieren wir oder spielen unentschieden. In meiner Freizeit spiele ich auch im Park neben dem Haus Fußball. Außerdem schaue ich auch Fußballspiele im Fernsehen. Manchmal nimmt mein Vater mich mit ins Stadion, wo wir einem Spiel unseres Lieblingsvereins „Hamburger SV" zuschauen. Ich mag den Spieler Paulo Guerrero, aber ich glaube: Zur Zeit ist Cristiano Ronaldo der beste Fußballspieler der Welt.

2. I like watching football (soccer). But I don't play it myself. My favourite hobby is basketball. I play in a club, which is called "BC Rebound". I go to the training twice a week (Tuesday and Thursday). At weekened we usually have matches against other teams.

23

1. **a)** My last weekend was eventful. **b)** The weather was unsettled. From time to time it rained, then the sun shone again. **c)** On Saturday I helped my father in the garden. **d)** Then my family and I went shopping in the city. **e)** Later on I played computer games. **f)** On Sunday morning the whole family went to church. **g)** Next we had lunch at a restaurant. **h)** After that my friend and I visited a fair. **i)** In the evening I watched TV. **j)** The best thing of the weekend was the visit of the fair.

2. At the fair we had a lot of fun. We went on a roller coaster and in a ghost train. Finally my friend and I had a ride on a merry-go-round.

24

1. **a)** Seife; **b)** Zahnpasta; **c)** Shampoo; **d)** Haarspray; **e)** Haartonikum, Haarstärkungsmittel; **f)** Frisierlotion; **g)** Rasiercreme; **h)** Körperspray; **i)** Gesichtscreme; **j)** Gesichtswasser; **k)** Augenstift, Kajalstift; **l)** Lippenstift; **m)** Nagellackentferner; **n)** Creme; **o)** Mundwasser; **p)** Duschgel; **q)** Haargel; **r)** Haarfärbemittel; **s)** Haarentferner; **t)** Rasierwasser; **u)** Schminke, Make-up; **v)** Gesichtspuder; **w)** Wimperntusche; **x)** Lidschatten; **y)** Nagellack

29 The answers

24

2. I use soap, toothpaste, mouthwash, shampoo, shower gel, hair gel, shaving cream, aftershave, body spray.
3. I don't like piercings, tattoos and body paintings.
4. **a)** I wash my face. **b)** I brush my teeth. **c)** I put on my pullover. **d)** I dye my hair. **e)** I comb my hair. **f)** I shave my beard. **g)** I rinse my mouth. **h)** I cut my fingernails. **i)** I put on some body lotion.

25

1. **a)** Yes, I am. **b)** I go shopping once or twice a week. **c)** My favourite colours are white, black, red and green. **d)** I like to wear modern shirts, trousers and pullovers. **e)** **XS** = extra small, **S** = small, **M** = medium, **L** = large, **XL** = extra large, **XXL** = extra extra large **f)** My size is medium. **g)** I don't like wearing skirts and coats. **h)** Yes, I am. **i)** No, I wouldn't. **j)** Well-dressed people are often more successful in their lives.

26

1. Good for health: going for sports, eating fruits, going to the doctor, reducing overweight, riding a bicycle, eating vegetables
   Bad for health: smoking cigarettes, playing computer games every day, eating lots of chips, drinking alcohol, drinking coke, watching TV all day long
2. **a)** To go jogging, to avoid stress. **b)** To use drugs like hashish, herion, marihuana, ... To eat fatty meals.
3. I go for sports (swimming, jogging, gymnastics) and I eat lots of fruits and vegetables.
4. Fruits (for example apples) are good for health. You should eat them every day.
5. Individuelle Lösungen!

27

1. friendly, tidy, reliable, reserved, curious, polite, helpful, honest, sensitive, jolly
2. **a)** nervous; **b)** angry; **c)** sad; **d)** bored; **e)** lucky; **f)** disappointed; **g)** happy; **h)** funny; **i)** proud; **j)** in love
3. your mother, your sister, your friend, a policeman, your neighbour, your father, your brother, other pupils, a trainer, your teacher
4. Girls: pay more attention to their clothes, get better marks at school, love dancing, are more romantic, have egg cells
   Boys: are more aggressive, can run faster, play football, cause more troubles, have a penis
5. Excuse, can you help me? Can you tell me what time it is? Are you here for the first time? Would you like a drink? Would you like to dance? Do you have a little time for me? You have got beautiful eyes. May I see you again? May I ask you for your telephone number? Would you like to go for a walk?
6. baby, candy, honey, sugar, sweetheart, bunny, darling, mouse, sugar baby, sweetie
7. It's really true:
I love you.

   Your eyes are blue
and I need you.

   Your lips are red,
can't get you out of my head.

   I love you forever,
hope to loose you never.

   You figure is cool
Let's go swimming in the pool.

   Just from the start
you're in my heart.

   You look so fine –
will you be mine?

   You're nice and kind
always in my mind.

   It's very fine,
your are my sunshine.

   Baby, you are funny,
I'd love you to be my bunny.
8. parents, sports, music, weather, jobs, friends, politics, love, school, violence
9. in love; beautiful; "All you need is love"; get lovesick; like many kisses; like petting; can have sexual intercourse; **h)** that the woman gets pregnant; can be a wonderful feeling; is a very serious disease
10. The body changes from being a child to being an adult. The female breast starts growing. Young women begin to menstruate. The male voice gets deeper (vocal change). Young men start producing sperms. Girls and boys fall in love. Many young people begin to smoke cigarettes and drink alcohol. Many teenagers come home later. Some of them have troubles with their parents. Many teenagers loose interest in school.

28

1. book, magazine, mobile phone, television, video recorder, newspaper, telephone, radio, computer, CD player
2. Advantages: The media offer entertainment, excitement and diversion. You are reachable at any place and any time. Media make people's life easier. You can get a lot of information in a short time. Computer is high technology.
   Disadvantages: Buying and using of media cost money. People can become aggressive. You can get addicted to media. Social contacts between people get lost. Some people loose contact to reality, they live in a virtual world.
3. My star is Otto Waalkes. He is a comedian. Otto was born in Emden, today he lives in Hamburg most of the time. His hair is long and blond, he is very tall. Otto is married for the second time. He has got one son from his first marriage. The comedian is about 60 years old. Anyway, he is still vital and funny. You can see Otto on stage and in films.
4. When is your birthday? How many brothers and sisters have you got? How did you like school? What were your favourite subjects at school? What are your hobbies now? What do you like to eat or drink? Where do you spend your holidays? What don't you like at all? Are you in love? What plans do you have for the future?
5. **a)** health; **b)** thinking and learning; **c)** achieving success; **d)** your self-confidence; **e)** reducing stress and aggressions; **f)** education; **g)** conversation and social contacts; **h)** experiences, events, adventures; **i)** diversion, entertainment and fun; **j)** a wonderful leisure activity
6. **a)** go shopping; **b)** go swimming; **c)** play football; **d)** play table tennis; **e)** visit a museum; **f)** visit friends; **g)** take pictures; **h)** dance; **i)** read a book; **j)** ride a bicycle
7. My hobby is music. I am very interested in music. Above all I like popular songs. At present my favourite song is .... Besides I like Hip-Hop and Raps. I hear music on the radio, walkman and MP3-player, ... You can say: Music is my life. I don't only listen to music, I also play music myself. I play the trumpet in a band. Finally I love dancing.

KOHL VERLAG Der Verlag mit dem Baum www.kohlverlag.de
English: quite easy / Band 6
All about teenagers - Bestell-Nr. 10 940

29 The answers

28

8. **a)** This weekend was very nice. **b)** The weather was warm and dry. **c)** On Saturday morning I got up at 10 a.m.. **d)** Then I had a shower and breakfast. **e)** Later on I went swimming. **f)** On Sunday morning I had a football match. **g)** At lunchtime we had pizza at home. **h)** After that I met some friends. **i)** At last we went to the cinema and watched a funny film. **j)** The best thing of my weekend was the party on Saturday evening.

9. **a)** soap; **b)** cream; **c)** toothpaste; **d)** shower gel; **e)** body spray; **f)** aftershave; **g)** make up; **h)** nail polish; **i)** lipstick; **j)** hair colour

10. **a)** Smoking cigarettes. **b)** Drinking alcohol. **c)** Drinking coke. **d)** Eating lots of chips. **e)** Playing computer games all day long. **f)** Eating vegetables. **g)** Eating fruits. **h)** Going for sports. **i)** Reducing overweight. **j)** Going to the doctor.

Let's talk

Arbeitsmaterial zur Dialogschulung *(5.-9. Schuljahr)*

„Let's talk" sind Dialogkarten für den Englisch-Unterricht in den Klassen 5-9. Dieses Arbeitsmittel zur Redemittelschulung besteht aus verschiedenen Dialogkarten mit einer deutschen Dolmetschanweisung, die ins Englische übertragen werden soll. Die Dolmetschkarten eignen sich sowohl zum Einsatz in Einzelarbeit als auch in Partner- oder Gruppenarbeit. Verschiedene methodische Umsetzungsmöglichkeiten sind ausführlich beschrieben. Der verwendete Wortschatz ist den jeweiligen Klassenstufen angepasst. Die Kopiervorlagen eignen sich besonders für das mündliche Englischlernen und zur Übung bzw. Vorbereitung für die veränderten mündlichen Abschlussprüfungen.

60 Kopiervorlagen **Nr. 10 951** **16,80 €**

Englisches Lesetraining - Sinnerfassendes Lesen mit Fremdsprachen

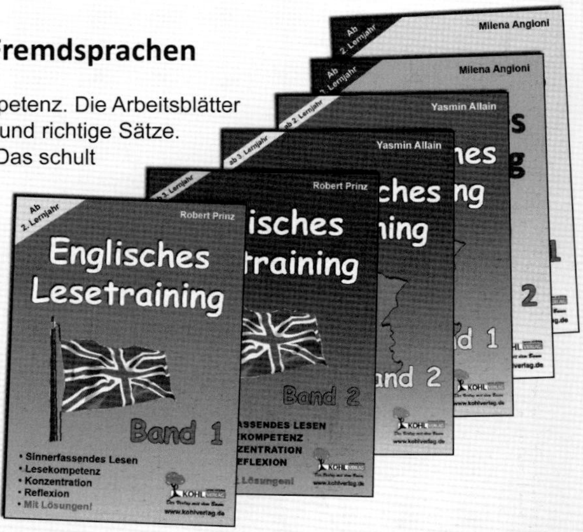

Die Lesetexte schulen den Umgang mit der Fremdsprache und dienen der Bildung von Lesekompetenz. Die Arbeitsblätter sind zweigeteilt: Auf der oberen Hälfte steht der zu lesende Text, die untere Hälfte enthält falsche und richtige Sätze. Der Schüler hat nun die Aufgabe (ohne erneut nachzulesen), die richtigen Sätze herauszufiltern. Das schult die Konzentration und das sinnerfassende Lesen! **Mit Lösungen zur Selbstkontrolle!**

Je 18 Lesetexte mit aufsteigendem Schwierigkeitsgrad.

• **Englisch**	- **Band 1** *(ab 2. Lj.)*	**Nr. 10 675**	**9,90 €**	**Beide: Nr. 40 019 nur 17,90 €**
	- **Band 2** *(ab 3. Lj.)*	**Nr. 10 676**	**9,90 €**	
• **Französisch**	- **Band 1** *(ab 2. Lj.)*	**Nr. 10 744**	**9,90 €**	**Beide: Nr. 40 020 nur 17,90 €**
	- **Band 2** *(ab 3. Lj.)*	**Nr. 10 745**	**9,90 €**	
• **Italienisch**	- **Band 1** *(ab 2. Lj.)*	**Nr. 10 758**	**9,90 €**	**Beide: Nr. 40 022 nur 17,90 €**
	- **Band 2** *(ab 3. Lj.)*	**Nr. 10 759**	**9,90 €**	

17 English Sketches

17 einfach zu spielende Szenen, vom 1. bis zum 4. Lernjahr einsetzbar. Das Anspruchsniveau der Stücke ist bewusst von unterschiedlichem Niveau. Es finden sich sowohl Stücke für Anfänger der englischen Sprache als auch welche für Fortgeschrittene im 3.-4. Lernjahr. Sketche sind ein hervorragendes Mittel zur Übung & Konzentration. Die Sketche eignen sich auch sehr gut zur Aufführung während eines Klassen- oder Elternabends!

44 Seiten **Nr. 10 071** **11,80 €**

Take it easy!

5-Minuten-Training Englisch

Hier sind **44 Kopiervorlagen** zu Grammatik, Wortschatz und Redewendungen. Mit einem **raffinierten Seitenstreifen**, der eine kinderleichte **Selbstkontrolle** ermöglicht! Take it easy! Ideales Material auch zum selbstständigen Üben! Einsetzbar im 1.-3. Lernjahr. Auch zum häuslichen Üben geeignet.

48 Seiten **Nr. 11 224** **13,80 €**

DO-DID-DONE

Die unregelmäßigen Verben

Das regelmäßige Üben der unregelmäßigen Verben ist unverzichtbar. Hier wurden Gruppen von Verben zusammengefasst, deren Stammformen Gemeinsamkeiten aufweisen. Nach dem Übungsteil wird das Blatt geknickt, nun gilt es, einen Lückentext zu vervollständigen. **10 Kopiervorlagen, mit Lösungen!**

Nr. 10 440 **6,90 €**

Bildungsstandard Englisch

Was 12-Jährige wissen und können sollten!

NEU!

Was sollten 12-Jährige vor dem Sprung ins nächste Schuljahr wissen und können? Wo weisen Ihre Schüler noch Wissenslücken auf? Die Kopiervorlagen geben Aufschluss über den Leistungsstand. Die Aufgaben können weitgehend selbstständig gelöst werden (sehr gut geeignet zur Nachhilfe!).

40 Kopiervorlagen, mit Lösungen!

Nr. 11 037** **12,80 €**

**Erscheint im Spätherbst 2009. Portofreie Nachlieferung!

Fremdsprachenunterricht

English – quite easy!

Elementares Fördermaterial Englisch

Englisch ist die Weltsprache Nummer Eins. Weltweit wird in der englischen Sprache im privaten und öffentlichen Leben kommuniziert. Englisch ist in vielfältigen Lebenssituationen anzutreffen. Die Sprache gilt als leicht zu erlernende Sprache, zumindest wird dies behauptet. Die Schulwirklichkeit jedoch zeigt: So manche Schüler haben sehr große Schwierigkeiten mit dem Englischen. Vor diesem Hintergrund entstand diese neue Lernreihe "English – quite easy", in der in kleinen Schritten ("step by step") vorgegangen wird. Diese Übungsreihe ist vorgesehen für Anfänger im Erlernen der englischen Sprache, sie ist konzipiert für den elementaren Förderunterricht. Die Kopiervorlagen gingen hervor aus der Schulpraxis – und zwar aus der langjährigen Arbeit mit Haupt- und Förderschülern. Jetzt sind zwei weitere Bände erhältlich!

je 12,90 €

- **Let's start to speak English** — **Nr. 10 805**
  (46 Kopiervorlagen, mit Lösungen)
- **Let's go on speaking English** — **Nr. 10 806**
  (46 Kopiervorlagen, mit Lösungen)
- **Grammar for beginners** — **Nr. 10 848**
  (48 Kopiervorlagen, mit Lösungen)
- **From Germany to the UK** — **Nr. 10 849**
  (48 Kopiervorlagen, mit Lösungen)
- **All about jobs** — **Nr. 10 939**
  (48 Kopiervorlagen, mit Lösungen)
- **All about teenagers** — **Nr. 10 940**
  (48 Kopiervorlagen, mit Lösungen)

Die Vokabel-Trainer Englisch

Den englischen Grundwortschatz spielerisch erweitern

Beide Bände: Nr. 40 089 nur 25,90 €

In diesen Bänden werden die jeweils passenden Begriffe des Grundwortschatzes gelernt, gesichert, wiederholt und vertieft. Auf spielerische Weise wird dadurch der Wortschatz erweitert. Die zahlreichen Dominos, Memories, Puzzles und Übungsaufgaben sind schulartübergreifend optimal einsetzbar!

Band 1 *(1.-3. Lernjahr)* **Nr. 10 823** **15,80 €**
(62 Kopiervorlagen, mit Lösungen)

Band 2 *(4.-5. Lernjahr)* **Nr. 10 828** **13,80 €**
(44 Kopiervorlagen, mit Lösungen)

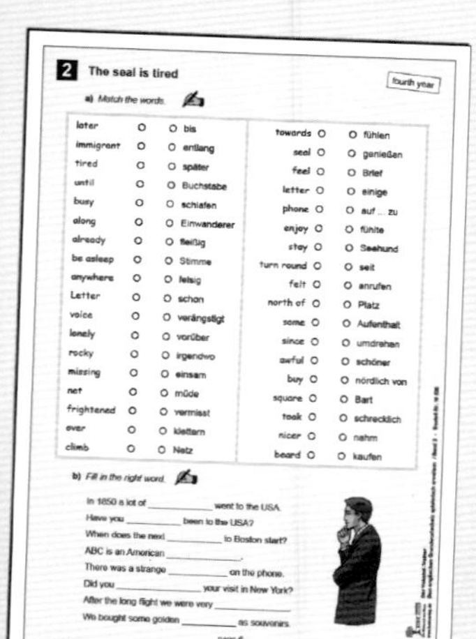

Belobigungsstempel

Eine positive Rückmeldung für gute Arbeit setzt zusätzliche Motivation frei! Machen Sie Ihren Schülerinnen und Schülern eine Freude!

„Very good"
Nr. 14 141 4,90 €

„Très bien"
Nr. 14 200 4,90 €

„Well done"
Nr. 14 206 5,90